The King and I

An Unlikely Journey from Fan to Friend

Howdy Giles

TRIUMPH
BOOKS

Library of Congress Cataloging-in-Publication Data

Giles, Howdy.
 The king and I / Howdy Giles.
    p. cm.
 ISBN 978-1-60078-285-5
 1. Palmer, Arnold, 1929- 2. Golfers—United States—Biography. I.
Title.
 GV964.P3G55 2009
 796.352092—dc22
 [B]

                          2009017492

This book is available in quantity at special discounts for your group or organization. For further information, contact:
 Triumph Books
 542 South Dearborn Street
 Suite 750
 Chicago, Illinois 60605
 (312) 939-3330
 Fax (312) 663-3557
 www.triumphbooks.com

Printed in U.S.A.
ISBN: 978-1-60078-285-5
Design by Wagner Donovan Design
Photos courtesy of the author

FOREWORD

How often have you heard somebody described as "one of a kind"? I think just about everybody has hung such a tagline on a person or two of their acquaintanceship. I know that I have...quite a few times over these many years, in fact. Mark McCormack, my longtime business manager and close friend, was a brilliant, one-of-a-kind person. So was my talented course-design partner, Ed Seay, and the boisterous sportswriter who covered my career from the start, Bob Drum.

Yet nobody has ever fit that description better than Howdy Giles, whose omnipresence and photographic talents made this book possible. I've had hundreds of people tell me that somebody they know is my No. 1 fan, and I certainly appreciate that kind of support. But I'm afraid that none of them can make a case that would take that distinction away from Howdy.

It seems so long ago that my late wife, Winnie, introduced me to Howdy and Carolyn Giles after she met them. She learned how big a fan of mine the young dentist and amateur photographer really was. Because his boundless enthusiasm struck a special chord with me, I encouraged him to be a friend as well as a fan. It got so I always knew that when Howdy and his ever-present camera were on the scene, my day would be recorded and preserved on hundreds of rolls of film.

What you will discover in this book is a unique and fairly complete photographic chronicle of my career and personal life back to the early 1970s. I believe the readers will get the same pleasurable memories that I did as they leaf through this attractive book.

Arnold Palmer

INTRODUCTION

The Field General of Arnie's Army

By James Dodson

On a cold, snowy afternoon in late 1996, I was sitting with my childhood sports hero, Arnold Palmer, and his wife, Winnie, in their penthouse suite on top of a famous Boston hotel. I'd been invited by the Palmers to attend the annual Francis Ouimet dinner and to chat privately with them beforehand about the prospect of helping "the King of Golf" write his long-awaited autobiography.

"People have been after me for years to write my book," Arnold said, scowling enough to let me know what he basically thought of such a prospect. "The idea of writing my autobiography, I have to say, doesn't appeal to me much at all. But Jack's [Nicklaus] just written his, so I guess I now have to write mine, too."

"In that case, maybe you shouldn't do your autobiography," I said. "Maybe you should write a memoir instead."

Arnold looked surprised. "What's the difference?"

I explained that an autobiography was typically a detailed account of one's life, whereas a "memoir" was a more selective and generally more relaxed literary form of telling one's own story. A memoir relied less on the delineation of chronological facts and more specific moments that revealed the essence of a life.

"Speaking purely as a reader and a fan," I amplified, "I'd like to read a book that sounds as if we are merely sitting together having a cocktail after a round of golf and you are speaking directly to me about the very personal things that shaped your life—the events, the people, and selected moments that determined what you accomplished, what you became. Who you really are."

"I like that approach," Winnie said, glancing at her husband. "How about you, Arn?"

The scowl vanished a bit. The King nodded as if he could see the value of such an approach.

"In some ways," I felt obliged to explain, "a memoir can be even more revealing than an autobiography because it explores important aspects of your life in intimate detail, the good and the bad, the successes as well as the adversity you've overcome. Given the intimacy your fans feel with you," I concluded my pitch, "I think that may be the way to go. The more you reveal about yourself, when all is said and done, the closer they'll feel to you."

Winnie agreed. Arnold nodded. "Fair enough," he said. "Let's get started."

As we rode the elevator downstairs to the ballroom where the Ouimet banquet was just getting under way, Winnie took my arm and said, "You know, you're so right about the intimacy Arnie enjoys with his fans. There's someone you need to meet and get to know right away. Their friendship says a lot about who Arnie really is."

The King looked at his wife and smiled. "You mean Howdy, I presume."

She smiled back at her husband. "Exactly. You have to admit, it is a remarkable friendship. I've never heard of anything else quite like it."

Arnold nodded and chortled, "That it is, babe. If you don't believe it, just ask Howdy."

This wasn't the first time I'd heard Dr. Howard "Howdy" Giles' name. I'd read in various golf publications that he was both Arnold Palmer's dentist and de facto photographer, "the field general of Arnie's Army," as one recent headline summed up the unique nature of the relationship.

A few weeks later, I met Howdy at the Bay Hill Club in Orlando, Florida. A rangy, grinning, relentlessly upbeat character armed with a camera was circulating through a small cocktail party at Arnold and Winnie's condominium, holding up an index finger to give his subjects a focus point. His camera flashed, it seemed like, every five or six seconds.

"In case you couldn't tell, that's Howdy," Winnie said with a laugh, and moments later Arnold's biggest fan and I shook hands. A few seconds after that, the dude snapped my photograph.

The next morning, I met Howdy and his lovely wife Carolyn for breakfast and began a conversation that quickly blossomed into a genuine friendship. As Winnie said, Howdy and Carolyn were two of the most likeable, unpretentious, easygoing folks you could ever meet. I asked Howdy if it was true that he'd built what amounted to a shrine to his hero Arnold Daniel Palmer in the basement of his home in Wilmington, Delaware.

"Oh, it's absolutely true," Carolyn answered. "You'll have to come see it to believe it. We've had Arnie with us our entire married life."

"You have no idea how fortunate I am," Howdy elaborated. "When I was growing up, like a million young guys in America, Arnold Palmer was the reason I started playing golf. I dreamed about meeting him someday. I even dreamed of maybe even somehow playing golf with him. Truthfully, I never really thought that could happen. But on the other hand,

this is America, where amazing things happen every day. Who knew that down the road a bit, through a number of unexpected connections, I would not only meet Arnold Palmer but become his dentist, friend, and photographer? It's an amazing story," he added, showing genuine emotion. "Only in America. I still wake up every day and pinch myself."

I asked Howdy to tell me the story. In 1962 a fraternity brother of Howdy's at Temple University invited him out to play a round of golf. Howdy was in dental school at the time and was not a golfer.

"My father was crazy about golf, but frankly the game never appealed to me much until I turned on the TV and there was Arnold Palmer playing in a golf tournament. The more I watched him, the more I realized golf was really pretty cool—at least the way he played it.

"Arnie made golf look like such fun. So I went out with my buddy and played. After that, anytime Arnold was playing on TV, I was absolutely glued to the TV set. Like millions of others, there was something about him that seemed so decent and genuine. He was like somebody you might know from the old neighborhood."

In December 1963, Carolyn and Howdy were engaged to be married. For an engagement gift, Carolyn presented Howdy with a set of Wilson Arnold Palmer signature irons. Howdy already owned a set of Palmer woods. "By then I was completely hooked on golf—and everything Arnold Palmer. I went down to Wanamaker's department store in Philadelphia and bought the same Robert Bruce shirts, sweaters, and pants that Arnie wore. I had the same kind of shoes he wore. I even began collecting anything that had his name on it. To millions of guys like me, Arnie just seemed to define what was great about the game of golf."

In 1965 a fraternity brother named Pete Richter invited Carolyn and Howdy to watch the Miss America parade in Atlantic City, New Jersey. Arnold Palmer was the parade's grand marshal.

"We were sitting in box seats right down by the parade route when along comes Arnie, Winnie, and the girls in a Cadillac convertible. I had my little Brownie camera with me. I yelled, 'Hey, Arnie!' and he looked over. That's when I snapped his picture. He was looking right at me, grinning. It almost felt like he recognized me! But that's a feeling Arnie gives to many of his fans."

Within a year, Howdy had graduated from dental school and joined the navy. He was stationed at the San Diego Naval Hospital, practicing his trade by day and practicing his game by night at an all-night driving range. When he heard Arnold would be playing in the 1967 L.A. Open, he bought a ticket to the tournament and followed his hero around every step of the way. Carolyn carried his new Nikon camera in her handbag. "On Sunday, there we are at the 12th hole. Arnie has a one-stroke lead and a 30-footer for birdie. I take out the camera, the red light comes on, and he knocks in the putt to take a two-shot lead just as I snap the picture."

Palmer went on to beat Gay Brewer by five strokes. When the press photographers snapped photographs of the charismatic winner, runner-up, and low amateur, Dr. Howdy Giles was squatting at the front of the pack, capturing his own images of the moment.

Ironically, though he would go on to follow Arnold Palmer in more than 200 tournaments and championships, this would be the only time Howdy ever saw him win in person.

A year later, Howdy and Carolyn attended their first Masters—the one where Arnie missed his first cut ever.

In 1970, though, a mutual friend invited Howdy—now back in Delaware running his own dental practice—to meet his hero at the World Putting Championship being staged at the Arnold Palmer Putting Course in Spring Lake, Delaware. "There were a couple thousand fans on hand, but I finally got introduced to Arnie as he was going in. He was great. When I asked if I might get a picture with him, he didn't hesitate. Darrell Brown, his pilot, took the picture. I was on cloud nine."

Six months later, at the Masters of 1971, an Augusta TV executive named Bert Harbin introduced Howdy and Carolyn to Winnie Palmer. The Palmers rented Harbin's house during Masters week for almost 25 years.

"She couldn't have been nicer to Carolyn and me," Howdy remembers. "When we explained to her that we were planning to drive on down to Bay Hill after the Masters, hoping maybe to see Arnold there, she apologized and explained that she and Arnold planned to go home to Latrobe that next week. The next day, though, she found us in the huge crowd by the 13th hole and told us that she'd arranged for Dick Tiddy, the head pro at Bay Hill, to take full care of us. It was such an incredibly thoughtful gesture on her part—the kind of thing you never forget."

One evening while the Gileses were dining at Bay Hill, the maitre d' moseyed over to ask how they were enjoying their stay at the club, noting that "Mrs. Palmer" had phoned from Latrobe to "make sure they were having a good time."

"That's it," Howdy told his bride. "Whatever it takes, we're going to join Bay Hill."

When Howdy and a friend played in their first Bay Hill Member-Guest Tournament in 1973, none other than Arnold Palmer paid $650 to purchase their team in the tournament Calcutta. "I think he felt sorry for us. We were the last team purchased," Howdy said with a sheepish grin. "I paid Arnie $300 to buy half of our team back. We started out great, shooting 67 in the opening round. Unfortunately, we finished in second-to-last place."

One evening during the tournament, the Gileses were invited over to the Palmers' for cocktails. "I remember remarking to Carolyn as we walked over to Arnold and Winnie's place that something like this could only happen in America. It was like there were two Arnold Palmers: the icon and the golf star, and Arnie, the ordinary guy. Obviously they were one in the same, and in the fullness of time that's what I came to realize about Arnold Palmer—and why he has such a magnetic pull on people.

"He is exactly as he appears, one of the most comfortable people in his own skin you'll ever meet. There's no façade, nothing artificial. He's as genuine as they come, and that quality is the key, I believe, to his incredible popularity, the reason he's as beloved today by millions as he was 50 years ago when he won his first Masters and created Arnie's Army."

As the colorful decade of the '70s unfolded, Howdy and Carolyn Giles became part of the living tapestry of interesting people who were part of Arnold and Winnie's private lives. They received Christmas cards and attended the Presidential Ball at Latrobe Country Cub every year with the Palmers. They traveled out west to join the Palmers in Los Angeles and found themselves dining at the homes of Bob Hope and Jack Lemmon, included in fetes with movie stars and political luminaries. For the next 20 years, they became part of the small retinue of folks who traveled the circuit to support Arnie on and off the golf course.

By this point, Howdy had even become Arnold's regular dentist. "I was trained in the navy not to be nervous while working on the teeth of an admiral." Howdy quipped, "It wasn't a far leap to working on a king. Besides, Arnie was a great patient—though his bridgework did need some reworking. We did it all in stages."

All the while, Howdy's Nikon camera was working overtime, snapping both posed and intimate photographs of his hero and friend at 1,001 places along the busy Palmer highway of life, essentially photodocumenting Arnold Palmer's remarkable journey both on and off the golf course.

As the '80s dawned, upon the supportive recommendation of Arnold, Howdy became a USGA official and worked his first USGA Junior and Senior Open championships. His first U.S. Open Championship as a rules man came in 1987. It was during this period of time that Howdy began regularly flying to the Masters with Arnold and meeting the first of several U.S. presidents, all of whom were as smitten as he was with Arnold Palmer. Howdy became famous for his raised index finger, a posture created to give his subjects a focal point for a photograph, and a camera shutter that was never at rest for long.

When friends gathered in Latrobe to celebrate the King of Golf's 50th, 60th, and 70th birthdays, Howdy and Carolyn were there. When Arnold bade good-bye to his tournament career at Oakmont in 1994, followed by his poignant fare-thee-well to the British Open at St. Andrews in '95, Brother Howdy captured the historic moments on film. Dozens of his images found their way to the covers of golf and sports publications around the world, into newspapers, tournament programs, and personal scrapbooks of the King's loyal servants. Famed artist LeRoy Nieman even used one of Howdy's most celebrated snaps as the basis for his portrait of golf's most charismatic figure.

The obvious affection went both ways, though. When Howdy's oldest daughter, Robin, got married in the winter of 1997, Arnold and Winnie flew through a blizzard to reach the big event in Delaware. Two years later, with Winnie gamely battling cancer, Howdy's camera captured the intimate group of close friends and family who gathered to celebrate both Arnold's birthday and the opening of the handsome old red barn just off the 16th hole at Latrobe Country Club, something Winnie had hoped to live long enough to see completed. Not long afterward, they returned to say good-bye to Winnie.

When Arnold bade farewell to the Masters in 2004, Howard "Howdy" Giles busily recorded every moment of it on his Nikon camera. When Arnold and Kit came to Bay Hill from their surprise marriage on a beach in Hawaii that next winter, Howdy got the first photograph of the smiling newlyweds.

On New Year's Eve a few years ago, Mark McCormack, the founder of the powerful International

Management Group and Arnold's longtime agent, asked Howdy how much he got paid for his photographs that found their way to the pages of magazines and commercial products.

"Oh, I don't know," Howdy replied in his usual low-key style. "Maybe a $1,000 or so."

"That's not nearly enough," McCormack told him.

As it happened, a company called AriZona Tea had just secured a number of Howdy's photographs of Arnold for the label of its soon-to-be-launched Palmer Iced Tea product.

"Tell me something else. How many pictures of Arnold have you taken over the past 50 years?" McCormack followed up.

Howdy replied that he couldn't be sure. But it was roughly a quarter of a million photographs.

"So, in effect, you have a photographic history of Arnold's life," McCormack said. "Look, Howdy, we should do a book of your photographs. I'm going to make that my next big project. We'll have it in time for Arnold's 80th birthday."

A short time later, though, McCormack went in for elective surgery, suffered a stroke, and died. The idea sat idle for at least three years. But Howdy Giles' camera never stopped. What you have before you is a book Mark McCormack and Winnie Palmer would both have loved to have seen.

The King and I is the visual fruit of one of the most remarkable and perhaps unlikely friendships in all of American sports. It is essentially an insider's snapshot-by-snapshot history of Palmer's public and private life almost from the moment he burst on the national sporting scene to today. It is a dedicated fan's scrapbook to his all-American hero. It is Arnold at work and at play, unfiltered and unplugged.

If it's true that a picture is worth a thousand words, we also have the benefit of hearing in Howdy's own words the often intriguing story behind the photographs, the sometimes amusing and heartfelt behind-the-scenes details that made the moment so unique and special.

As you browse through these pages, watching Arnold Palmer grow gracefully older with the rest of the golf-mad generations he inspired over the past half-century, you'll also hear the voices of other well-known figures who shared Howdy's huge affection for the King of Golf and frequently found themselves the subject of his camera.

"I think Howdy Giles was a godsend to us," Winnie Palmer remarked to me as we drove in the hills around Latrobe one beautiful autumn afternoon not long before she passed away. "He can drive you crazy with that finger held up and that camera of his constantly going off—I personally hate having my picture taken—but I wouldn't trade Howdy and Carolyn for anything. They've been great friends to have along the way.

"Howdy not only brings out the best in Arnold, but I also think he perfectly reflects the unique relationship Arnold has with his fans," she added. "Arnie loves life and appreciates everything that has come his way. He cares deeply about people, and that quality comes across in Howdy's photographs."

She looked at me and then laughed, sounding almost girlish.

"He even loves Howdy, too—even though he grumbles about him taking way too many pictures of him."

THE 1960s

THE KING won all except one of his professional major championships and 55 of his 92 career victories around the world on his way to being designated the Associated Press Athlete of the Decade.

AND I started dental school in 1962. In the '60s Arnold Palmer was *the king*. As a dental student, I dreamed that I would meet Arnold Palmer, that I would play golf with him, and that someday I would become his dentist.

1965: A Fan Is Born

I'm what you'd call the ultimate fan, as you will see. Arnie had been chosen as the grand marshal for the Miss America Pageant parade in September 1965. Friends had invited Carolyn and me to join them, and suddenly there he was, waving to the crowd and smiling that I'm-truly-glad-you're-here smile. As he passed by, I yelled, "Hey, Arnie," and he looked over—I thought just at me. I snapped this picture, and in that moment a fan was born.

Dreams come true in Atlantic City.

MISS AMERICA
1965

The result: one of my earliest photos of Arnie. His winner's take was $20,000. Here he is with runner-up Gay Brewer (left) and the low amateur (center).

Frenzied Spectator Becomes Sports Photographer

In January 1966 I had graduated from dental school and was stationed at the naval hospital in San Diego. Arnie was leading the L.A. Open at Rancho Park, and Carolyn and I went to watch him play in person for the first time. It was a first for us; I had only ever seen him play on TV. Going into the final round, he led by one stroke. As he putted for a birdie on 12, I grabbed my camera from Carolyn's purse and snapped a photo of him sinking the putt that gave him a two-shot lead. He eventually won the tournament by four shots over Gay Brewer. Afterward, I got caught up in the frenzy of sports photographers taking pictures of the winners. I joined them and continued to snap away.

Connecticut, 1967

In mid-1967, I was transferred from San Diego to the USS *Fulton*, a submarine tender in New London, Connecticut. In September, I entered a local golf tournament at Shennecossett Golf Club and shot a gross 77 with a 15 handicap for a net 62. I won by 4 shots and was ecstatic.

Carolyn was starting to share my somewhat over-the-top obsession with golf in general and Arnold Palmer in particular. To celebrate, she took the Palmer umbrella logo from a glove and attached it to the visor I used in the tournament (along with my AP clubs). And as a victory gift she gave me Mark McCormack's book about Arnie, *The Evolution of a Golfer*. I had no idea where it would lead, but I was loving every minute of it.

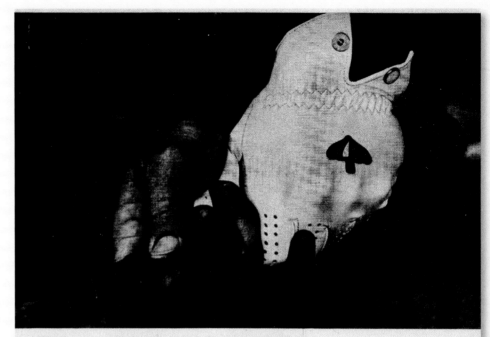

Play without this glove? Arnie would rather play without shoes.

"WHEN you use a golf glove as much as I do," says Arnold Palmer, "you shouldn't even know you're wearing one."

That's why Arnie developed this great glove. It's made of beautiful Cabretta leather. The grain is close (which makes it lighter) and it has a marvelous tacky feel. (*Tacky*, not sticky.)

Arnie put wide, cushioned elastic across the back of the hand and along the inside of the wrist. That keeps the leather from bunching up and binding.

The stitching is nylon. It doesn't give and it won't rot from dampness. (The double holes in the fingers help your hand breathe, too.)

Arnie even put the seams on the inside (where they belong) so they're not exposed to sunlight.

(Sunlight is death to nylon.)

When Arnie makes a glove and plays tournament golf with it you can bet your last golf ball it's the best there is. Anywhere. Pick one up at your pro shop and play a round or two. If your game improves, credit yourself. Not the glove. (That's okay with us.)

Arnold Palmer Golf Company, Chattanooga, Tennessee

SOLD BY GOLF PROFESSIONAL SHOPS ONLY
MANUFACTURED AND DISTRIBUTED IN CANADA BY CAMPBELL

Arnie's own.

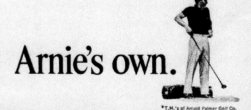

*T.M.'s of Arnold Palmer Golf Co.

The glove.

Me dressed up in my umbrella hat and glove and holding my Arnold Palmer club.

Carolyn attempts to gently convey to our firstborn, Robin, that Palmer memorabilia is going to be important in the life of our family.

April 1968: Springtime Among the Azaleas

I think I was born under a lucky star. Golfers everywhere were jostling to get tickets to the Masters, and our request was honored on our first try. I've come to love golf tournaments in general, but there's something magical about Augusta in April. Arnie won a total of four Masters, and to be able to watch him play there was another dream come true.

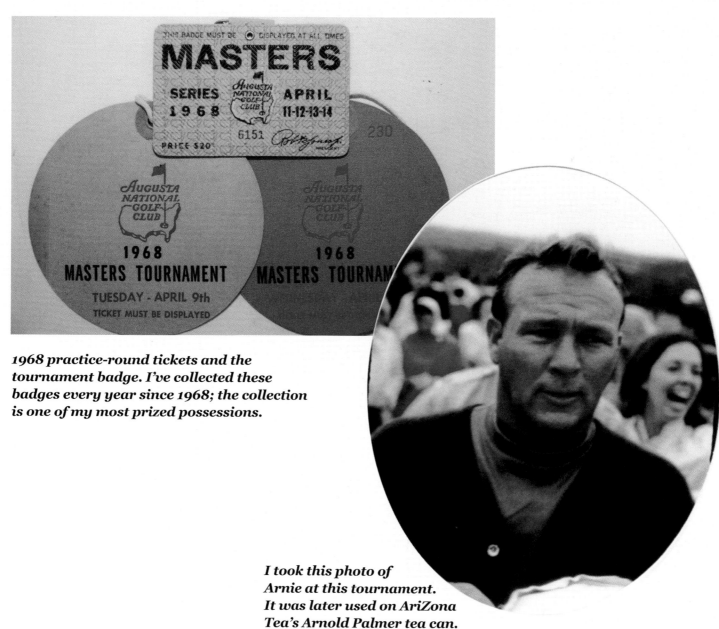

1968 practice-round tickets and the tournament badge. I've collected these badges every year since 1968; the collection is one of my most prized possessions.

I took this photo of Arnie at this tournament. It was later used on AriZona Tea's Arnold Palmer tea can.

Arnie practicing on the putting green during a practice round that year. Am I lucky or what?!

THE 1970S

THE KING was winding down his play on the PGA and other tours. Meanwhile, he was building his course-design operations with Ed Seay into a flourishing worldwide business.

AND I saw all my Arnold Palmer dreams become a reality. My wife and I met Arnie in October 1970, played golf with him in May 1976, and welcomed him to the dental office in October 1978.

First Fan Photo-Op

By 1970 I was back in Delaware practicing my dentistry and my golf. Watson Richards (the CEO of Atlantic Aviation) had promised to introduce me to Arnie if he ever came to Delaware. That opportunity occurred when Arnie came to Spring Lake, Delaware, where the World Putting Championship was being staged. As Arnie entered the championship area, we were introduced, and he graciously agreed to have a photo taken with us. This was my first up-front-and-personal meeting with him, and it was awesome.

My first face-to-face photo encounter with Arnie, who is standing next to Watson Richards. Arnie's pilot, Darrell Brown, took the picture.

Arnie greeted each Member-Guest participant and had photos taken with them and their wives outside the clubhouse prior to teeing off.

14 The King and I

November 1973: My First Bay Hill Member-Guest

Visiting the Bay Hill Club was so neat that we stretched our budget and joined. We attended our first Member-Guest in 1973 with my partner Dr. Cliff Anzilotti and his wife Sandy. Arnie bought our team for $650 in the Calcutta. We started strong, faded, and rewarded him by finishing 63rd in a group of 64 teams. While there, Carolyn and I had a photo taken with Arnie, which became that year's Christmas card to our golfing friends.

Arnie smiling after buying our team in the Calcutta. We already felt like the winners!

HOLIDAYJOY

Our golfing friends got a kick out of this card. Do we look happy or what?

Carolyn, Pete Richter (my partner) and his wife Pat, Danny Bonar (Arnie's insurance agent), Dr. Benny Tacke, and Arnie's No. 1 fan.

The Bay Hill Member-Guest 1974

Dr. Benny Tacke had been Arnie's dentist in Latrobe since Arnie was three years old. Benny and I shared lots of laughs together. I once told him that I always dreamed that someday I would be Arnie's dentist, and Benny jokingly replied, "When I die, you can have him." He died in 1977, but I'll always remember the fun times I had with him at those Member-Guests.

In a real turnaround, Pete and I finished first low gross and were congratulated by Arnie.

17

My first round with Arnie. On the left is Bob Kirby and on the right is Danny Bonar.

*Not too shabby
when you consider
I was shaking in
my shoes for much
of the round.*

HOLE	LONG (RED)	REGULAR (WHITE)	MEN'S PAR	HANDICAP	ARNOLD	HOWDY	MATCH + or −	DAN	BOB	LADIES (BLUE)	LADIES' PAR	LADIES' HANDICAP
										385	4	3
1	407	397	4	5	4	5		4	5	110	3	17
2	132	121	3	17	4	3		3	3	430	5	1
3	442	437	4	1	4	5		5	6	175	3	9
4	205	180	3	7	3	5		4	4	270	4	15
5	295	277	4	15	4	5		4	4	364	4	5
6	480	468	5	11	4	6		4	6	355	4	7
7	370	358	4	3	5	6		5	4	416	5	13
8	500	485	5	9	6	5		4	5	302	4	11
9	330	317	4	13	5	4		4	5			
Out	3161	3040	36		39	44		37	42	2807	36	
10	210	195	3	6	3	4		4	3	171	3	6
11	405	397	4	2	4	5		5	5	310	4	10
12	345	335	4	14	3	5		4	4	329	4	8
13	185	175	3	12	3	4		4	5	168	3	12
14	500	490	5	10	5	6		7	6	340	4	2
15	510	490	5	8	4	6		4	3	432	5	4
16	360	330	4	16	5	4		5	6	265	4	18
17	353	341	4	18	5	6		4	6	330	4	14
18	375	372	4	4	4	5		40	47	370	5	16
In	3243	3125	36		36	45		77	84	2715	36	
Total	6404	6165	72		75	89				5522	72	

DATE: SCORER: PLAYER:

The Quality of a Golf Club is Known by the Etiquette of its Members

May 22, 1976:
I Play My First
18-Hole Round of
Golf with Arnie

We were headed to the President's Ball at Arnie's Latrobe Country Club (we took a membership there, too). Danny Bonar called to say he'd arranged a foursome with Arnie on Saturday and invited me to play. I had a hard time sleeping the night before. After dressing, eating breakfast, and reading the paper, I lay back down in bed on my back so as not to wrinkle my slacks. I'd been up forever, but it was only 8:15, still almost six hours until tee time. Finally, we teed off at 2:00 PM Bob Kirby, the CEO of Westinghouse, was our fourth. Carolyn was filming the entire round, and I quietly admitted to Arnie that I was a nervous wreck. He put his arm around me and said, "Relax. Just have a good time." I did just that.

From Snapping to Snipping

During one of our visits to Latrobe, Arnie asked Lee Lauderback's (his pilot) wife to trim his hair. I earned all my spending money in high school, college, and dental school giving $1 haircuts to student friends. He reluctantly but jokingly let me have a go at it—and then returned the favor pretending to give me a trim. (Note: I didn't charge anything for this service. In fact, I should have offered to pay him for the pleasure of clipping the King.)

Shear delight trimming Arnie's hair.

Does Arnie's facial expression mean he'd rather be golfing?

The Palmer family (left to right): Peg, Winnie, Arnie, and Amy.

Here's an article that was in the July 1978 issue of Delaware Today magazine, which features my favorite room in the house.

Arnie can't believe his eyes when Carolyn shows him our basement, where a multitude of Palmer memorabilia is displayed.

Homestyles

AT THE OTHER END OF THE spectrum is the ultra-modern California style home of Carolyn and Howard Giles in Surrey Park, north of Wilmington. The new Cadillac Coupe de Ville and super sports car with the HOWDY license plate in the driveway only hint at what's inside the house: lots of space, an airy look accomplished by a lack of doors, cathedral ceilings and light colors.

The large white foyer opens to the right onto the spring green walls of the living room. Soft yellow, overstuffed sofas and chairs face white, smokey mirror-topped coffee and end tables on top of a plush pale carpet that picks up the greens, yellows and whites in the room. An abstract painting covers most of one wall, and an original brass floral sculpture by Hunter Malpass gracefully tops a white box pedestal. The whole room was designed by Malpass, who is an interior designer and metal sculptor in West Chester, Pennsylvania.

Through the living rooms one can see the den/bar area done in rich browns and deep blacks. A zebra print looks down on a heavy dark wood desk. On the plank floor is a *real* zebra skin. A small bar stands next to a floor-to-ceiling bookcase on a wall that borders the kitchen area that is large, open, modern and pleasant. Then there's the recreation room—cathedral ceiling with exposed beams, fireplace on one wall, windows on another.

Dr. Giles (Howdy) is a dentist. His internship at the Naval hospital in San Diego, California had some affect on the style of house the Giles chose to build here. They like to entertain and designed accordingly. In fact, they entertain some well-known people—the Philadelphia Eagles' Bill Bergey was recently there for dinner and to see slides Howdy took during a Jets game. This month, the Giles are expecting the Arnold Palmers.

That's right! The *golfing* Arnold Palmers. Arnie and Winnie are good friends of the Giles; in fact, golfing

pictures of the foursome are part of their unusual basement. Actually, unusual may be an understatement—there is an Astro-turf putting green there.

Howdy is an avid golfer and a faithful Arnold Palmer fan. When the idea of putting the green (hole, flag and all) in the basement occurred to him, Giles had Malpass back to design the room like the 19th hole. A long curved paneled bar is reflected in the background mirrors which are set off with glasses and pictures and albums full of Arnie-abilia. There's even a director-type bar chair with Palmer's name on it.

Carolyn gets in on the act, too. Though not as avid a golfer as Howdy, she knows her way around the fairways. She even has a small business of selling hand-painted skirts and summer wear. Winnie Palmer wore her unique skirt in a recent photo in Golf Digest.

The Giles like Surrey Park. "We're sorta suburban-type people" says Carolyn, adding that they both were raised in suburbs of Philadelphia. "Surrey Park is a young neighborhood. There're lots of children for the kids (Robin, 10; Julie, 7) to play with, to walk to school with. And it's not a real transient neighborhood. Everybody here in this area is the original builder. The neighbors—they work for DuPont, are lawyers, dentists... there's a physician across the street, a couple bankers—it's a rather stable neighborhood." Convenience to the shopping centers and his practice are added advantages she mentions.

They sound content; do the Giles ever think of moving? Howdy says no. "We're very happy in this area. We like to go to Hilton Head (South Carolina) for our vacations and we have a piece of land down there; if we ever build again, we might just build there, like a vacation home or something. So, I think we'll just stay right here."

14

Here's the lamp on my putting green.

Some like Picasso art;
I prefer Palmer art.

Visiting My Home

It probably won't come as a surprise that I have Arnold Palmer furniture in my home. The Lexington Furniture Company did a commemorative line of Palmer furniture, and our den is filled with many of the beautiful pieces from that line.

In addition, a friend of mine had a standing Palmer floor lamp custom-made for me. She watercolor-painted the shade and searched high and low for Palmer clubs to attach to the shaft. Winnie got wind of this, and Arnie agreed to give three woods from his personal collection— clubs he had used in competition that had the Dewey-decimal-like codes identifying their use still attached. It is one of my most cherished possessions.

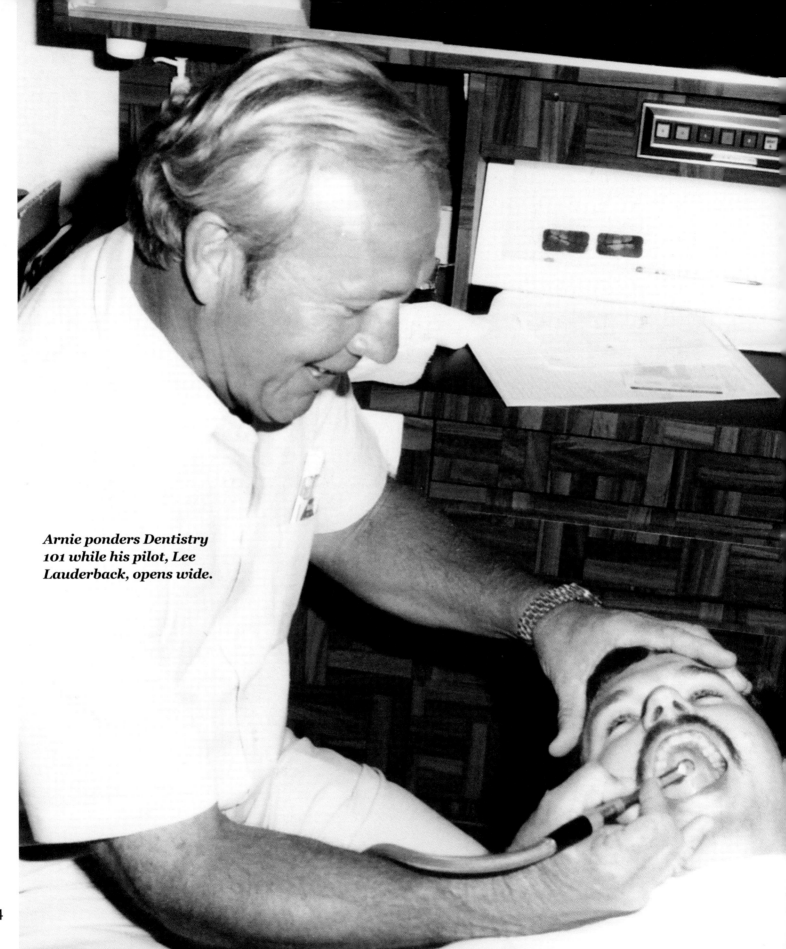

Arnie ponders Dentistry 101 while his pilot, Lee Lauderback, opens wide.

A sporting threesome when Bill Bergey joins us.

Visiting the Dental Office

Arnie's first visit to my dental office created quite a stir. (Many of my
friends jokingly call me "Dentist to the Stars.") One of my "star" patients,
Bill Bergey (All-Pro linebacker for the Philadelphia Eagles) asked to meet
Arnie because he was also a fan. Bill relayed to Arnie how, on his first
dental visit, all 250 pounds of him looked me in the eye and asked, "Now
we aren't going to hurt each other, are we?"

Arnie's first dental visit went so well that he decided that he was also good
with his hands and that he would probably make a good dentist. He had his
pilot, Lee Lauderback, sit in the chair. Then he had second thoughts…

Jeanette, Carolyn, and Bert join Winnie and Arnie for drinks.

As a dental follow-up, Arnie asks me to check his teeth, while Bert looks on.

1978 MEMBER-GUEST TOURNAMENT
Arnold Palmer's Bay Hill Club & Lodge

Our "formal" tournament portrait. Check out those pants!

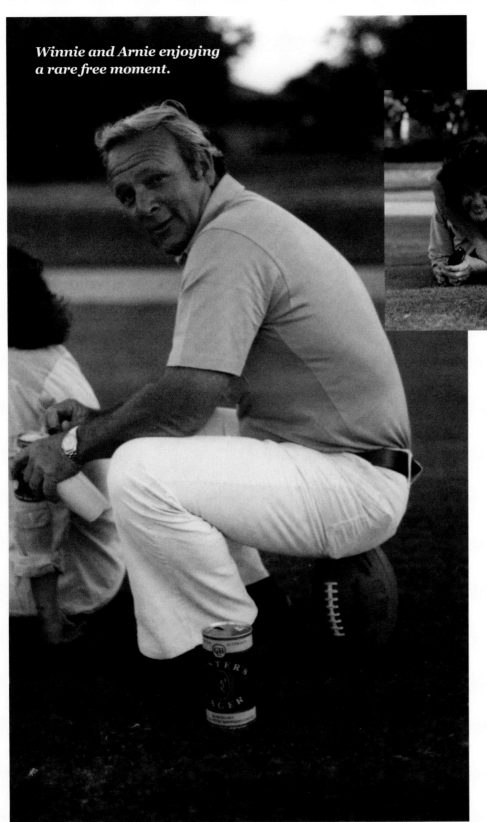

Winnie and Arnie enjoying a rare free moment.

October 1978: Another Memorable Bay Hill Member-Guest

Our guests at the Bay Hill Member-Guest in 1978 were Bert and Jeanette Harbin, who had introduced us to Arnie at the Masters in 1971. Winnie and Arnie rented their home for almost 20 years when they came to Augusta for the tournament.

Cowboy Arnie and his cowgirl Winnie.

Arnie and his cowpoke sidekicks.

Family members back at the ranch: Palmer's sisters Sandy and Lois Jean and brother Jerry.

The King Is 50! Long Live the King!

Arnie celebrated his 50th birthday in September 1979 in style—John Wayne style—at his home in Latrobe, surrounded by 70-plus family members and treasured friends. Guests were requested to dress in western garb, and Arnie set the pace wearing a 10-gallon hat. The picture I took of Arnie and Winnie cutting his birthday cake was picked up by *Golf World* for use in its article chronicling the festivities.

THE KING IS FIFTY; LONG LIVE THE KING

Arnold Palmer has residences in a lot of places, but home is still Latrobe, Pa., and that's where he celebrated his first half century.
By LARRY GUEST

Winnie gave Arnie a better grip for the cutting of the cake.

Though Arnold Daniel Palmer owns scattered homes and apartments and presently lists his Orlando Bay Hill Club for use in introductions on the No. 1 tees of the world, the heartbeat of the Palmer empire remains at the end of a private drive just across from Latrobe Country Club.

Three homes—Palmer's and those of two high-school chums—flank the little winding drive that climbs a gentle, wooded Western Pennsylvania hill overlooking the golf course and dead-ends at the door of Palmer's office. The quaint structure could be mistaken for a fourth home. But once through the white screen door, a visitor discovers a tidy configuration of cozy offices for Palmer, secretaries Carole Higgins and Kathy Constantine, "Man Friday" Doc Griffin, and Arnie's pilots. A short hallway leads into a spacious golf workshop where hundreds of clubs, bags, shoes and gloves are clustered in barrels and stacked against walls, workbenches and power tools.

The double doors to Palmer's personal office are almost always open, giving morning visitors an instant view of this international celebrity and making them privy to his non-stop telephone conversations.

A slight hearing deficiency pushes Palmer several decibels above the norm and his resonant bass tones reverberate throughout the small building.

"... and one of these days," he facetiously boomed into the receiver on a recent Monday morning, "I'm gonna learn how to play golf again and make a comeback."

On the other end of the line was a man in Dallas, one of a procession of friends and admirers who called all day and well into the night to extend best wishes on the occasion of Arnold Palmer's 50th birthday.

"Fifty??" he rebuked one caller, playfully feigning indignation. "There's no way I can be that old. Actually, I'm just 30 today. Somebody must have made a mistake." He laughed heartily. Carole and Kathy and Doc and a visiting sportswriter echoed a chorus of chuckles.

Palmer sat behind his memorabilia-laden desk looking something like an aging Christmas package. The casual green corduroy slacks and red pullover accented the thinning locks that are almost totally white now. No small child ever enjoyed a birthday more than Palmer on his half-century mark. On Sept. 10, he laughed and cajoled his staff and jovially bantered with callers and chased away the few quiet moments with a bar or two of whatever song came to mind. Once it was the pun punchline to an outrageous joke set to Tony Bennett's classic ballad. "I left My H-a-a-a-a-rp...," Arnie warbled. "In Sam Frank's Disco-o-o-..."

His birthday had begun and ended like all days when he's in Latrobe. The sun was barely peeking over Chestnut Ridge when the famous golfer-pilot took his usual two-mile jog through the golf course's early morning mist. He panted back through the door in time to complete the ritual by watching Arthur Smith pick his banjo from Charlotte—Arnie's favorite TV show.

"I was born at 5:30 on a Tuesday morning and I'm still getting started about that time every day," he mused.

Fourteen hours later, he would be commanding the bar in his comfortable basement den where some combination of neighbors, friends and employees assemble nightly.

The festivities had moved outside onto the driveway two nights earlier for a not-too-surprise, western-style birthday party, complete with a hay wagon ride for the 50 guests from the country club parking lot. What did surprise Arnie was the appearance of Arthur Smith, whom Winnie Palmer had flown in to perform. Smith, as much a fan of Arnie's as vice versa, refused Winnie's offer of pay. She had considered Glen Campbell, but "that would have meant an orchestra to back him up and I

18

The article that appeared in Golf World.

THE 1980S

THE KING was the linchpin who successfully launched and firmly established the PGA Senior (now Champions) Tour, winning 12 times, including five major championships.

AND I literally jetted around with Arnie and Winnie. In 1983 my family and I flew to Los Angeles for the PGA National Championship at Riviera. We met Bob Hope and Jack Lemmon. In 1986 Arnie asked us to fly to the Masters with him, a tradition we kept going until 2004.

Will the real dentist please stand up?

Arnie and Dallas

In 1980 the Philadelphia Phillies won the World Series with Dallas Green as manager. Arnie came for a dental appointment a short time later, and Dallas joined us for lunch. Back in the dental office, Arnie had Dallas sit in the patient chair for a candid photo with Arnie playing dentist. He got a big laugh. Arnie would always circulate throughout the office greeting staff and patients warmly. Talk about P.R.! This was as good as it gets.

Dr. Arnie and Dallas Green.

33

Howdy Meets Howdy Doody

One of Arnie's lifelong friends was Delvin Miller, part-owner of the Bay Hill Club, owner of the famed sulky Adios Club, and famous for participating in the trotters over eight decades. Delvin and his wife Mary Lib invited Carolyn and me to Delray Beach, Florida, to his Adios Club for a round of golf. Who was there in our foursome but another of his friends, Bob Smith (a.k.a. Buffalo Bob of Howdy Doody fame). We would later become friends ourselves, and we visited him in his Ft. Lauderdale home. Howdy and Howdy Doody under the same roof! When I asked to have my photo taken with the famous original Howdy Doody doll, Bob said that although the doll had not been out of its glass case in 20 years, an exception was about to be made. The photo was snapped, and Howdy Doody was quickly whisked back into his case. I now have my own collection of Howdy Doody memorabilia, but none of it means more to me than this photo.

Arnie with Buffalo Bob and his good friend Delvin Miller.

Howdy and Howdy Doody with Carolyn and Buffalo Bob.

Eagles vs. Oakland

The Philadelphia Eagles have always been an important part of my life. In 1980 I had seven Eagles as patients, including All-Pro middle linebacker Bill Bergey. Bill, an avid golfer, pleaded with me to schedule a dental visit with Arnie that would coincide with an Eagles game. In November 1980, we arranged an appointment for the day following the Eagles-Raiders game. Arnie and Winnie flew in Sunday morning, and we headed to the stadium for brunch with the owner, Leonard Tose. Afterward, we took a trip to the locker room, where Bill presented Arnie with an Eagles jersey featuring his No. 66 on the back. Bill was so flustered, he forgot his coach's name while introducing him to Arnie. We got to go out to the field to watch pregame warm-ups, where Tony Franklin, the Eagles' bare-footed place kicker, was practicing. Arnie asked him if he ever got nervous attempting a game-winning field goal. Tony replied by asking Arnie if he got nervous putting a two-footer to win the Masters. Touché! The day ended with a fabulous dinner at the Old Original Bookbinders. By the way, the Eagles won 10–7.

Carolyn and I have lots of memories to thank Bob Hope for...

Arnie, do you know the way to L.A.?

August 1983 PGA

One of the many highlights of our friendship with the Palmers was the opportunity to accompany them to the 1983 PGA Championship at Riviera Country Club in Los Angeles. We flew out on Monday night so Arnie would have a couple of days to practice. I was by his side, available for any task he needed.

On Wednesday night of tournament week, there was a cocktail party at Bob Hope's house. I knew Carolyn and Winnie were dying to attend. Luckily Arnie agreed, and it was a wonderful affair, followed by dinner at Chasen's in downtown L.A.

To top off the trip, we were invited to Jack Lemmon's house the following night. Jack was quite a fan of Arnie's, and he had such wonderful things to say about him. We ended up at a small restaurant in Santa Monica. As we were leaving the restaurant, Arnie put his arm around Carolyn and said, "You love this, don't you?!"

Arnie didn't win the tournament, but it was a winning week for us.

Cocktails at Jack Lemmon's. Better for us than Breakfast at Tiffany's! Pictured are Felicia and Jack Lemmon, Mac Dicker, Yvonne Hughes, Arnie, Carolyn, and Winnie.

TOOTH-ACE

The next time Arnold Palmer visits his dentist, he can rely on getting five-star treatment.

Why? His dentist, Howdy Giles, was playing in a tournament recently at Merion GC. The 129-yard 13th, one of Palmer's all-time favorites, was

continued

3/84 GOLF MAGAZINE 27

GOLF REPORTS *continued*

designated for closest-to-the-hole.

Well, Giles put his tee shot right into the cavity—using a set of irons given to him by Palmer the week before, and a ball presented by Palmer's wife, Winnie.

Tooth-Ace.

Arnie, Jack, and Howdy.

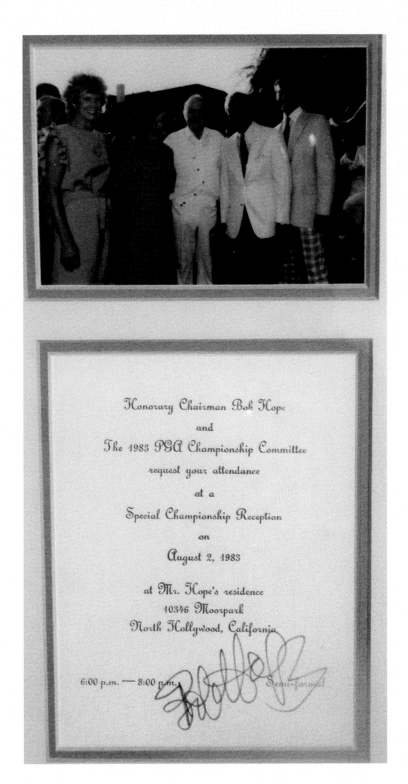

The Bob Hope invitation.

During our trip to L.A. for the PGA Championship, I was busy taking photos of Arnie while Winnie and Carolyn shopped. They stopped by a bank to get a new supply of cash, and when the bank president heard that Mrs. Palmer was there, he went to greet her. Before leaving he gave Winnie a sleeve of DT Titleists with the bank's logo. That evening Winnie gave me the balls. Within the month, Arnie sent me a new set of irons—"the Deacon," named for his father. Soon after, while playing in a tournament at Merion Golf Club, I had a hole-in-one on number 13 using the 9 iron from my new set and with one of the balls Winnie had given me. *Golf Magazine* wrote a clip about my good fortune and called it "Tooth-Ace."

(Note: It's funny that my ace occurred on Merion's 13th hole. This is one of the holes that appears on Arnie's list of his 18 favorite golf holes in the country.)

1983 Bay Hill Shootout

In Septemeber 1983, while playing in the Shootout at Bay Hill with Arnie, I was using a new driver I'd just gotten from the Arnold Palmer Golf Company, and Arnie asked to try it out. He smoked the ball down the fairway and asked if he cold borrow it to use in the first Senior Skins Game in Hawaii shortly thereafter. He promised that he'd return it, and he did just that. Some time later I was with Arnie when he was cleaning out his garage, and he asked if I'd like the pictured Johnston & Murphy Anteater golf shoes that he wore in this same Skins Game. Would I?!

These shoes were made for golfing...

Leukemia Golf Tournament

Arnie came to Wilmington, Delaware, in September 1987 to appear in an exhibition for the Leukemia Golf Tournament of Delaware, an event at which many local celebrities were to participate. My partners and I at Dental Associates of Delaware own a sports tavern (Stanley's) in Wilmington near our offices. Our owner-manager Steve Torpey had visors made with the Stanley's logo for the player participants, but I was reluctant to mention this to Arnie. But while he was boarding his jet to fly back to Latrobe, I asked if he would let me take his picture wearing the visor, saying we needed the photo for "promotional purposes." Arnie complied but added, "You don't need promoting. I spoke to your banker, and you're doing just fine!" The photo now hangs in a place of honor in Stanley's. (Note: One of the celebs playing that day was none other than the Phillie Phanatic.)

Arnie and the Phillie Phanatic.

Tug McGraw (Phillies pitcher and winner in the 1980 World Series, who threw the last pitch to win the last game), Bill Bergey, and Arnie .

Stanley's Restaurant

From left: Harry Anderson, Bill Bergey, Arnie, Dick Vermeil, Howdy, Pat Croce, and Dave Alexander.

Here's a shot I absolutely love. The year is 1988. The place is Stanley's Restaurant in my hometown of Wilmington, Delaware. Stanley's is a popular tavern-restaurant right across the street from my dental practice. Arnie had flown in for some dental work, and I proposed to him that we have lunch afterward over at Stanley's because I had some local buddies who were dying to meet him. He resisted a bit at first, pointing out how "numb" he would be from his time in the chair, but I came back that my pals wouldn't care a bit about that. They just wanted to meet the King! Arnie graciously relented, and here's the group photo I had a waiter take. This ordinary group of guys includes Eagles head coach Dick Vermeil, Pat Croce (president of the 76ers), Harry Anderson (right fielder for the Phillies), Bill Bergey (All-Pro linebacker for the Eagles), and Dave Alexander (center for the Eagles). Somehow an ordinary, grinning dentist got into the photo, too.

Arnie, Marge Yuengling, and Winnie.

Doc Murphey, Arnie, and Howdy.

Col. Joe Curtis and Arnie.

Tailgating in Augusta

Tailgating in the Masters' parking lot in Augusta is in a class by itself. In football, you tailgate with the same friendly folks who are rooting for your home team. Augusta is different. For one thing, you do it only once a year. For Arnie's Army of tailgaters, it always meant reconnecting with his most dedicated fans. After 20 to 30 to 40 years of being in his golf course gallery, Arnie was on a first-name basis with most of these loyal fans. There are some among this group I never want to forget.

Colonel Joe Curtis is a retired U.S. Air Force colonel who started following Arnie in 1956 and saw him win the U.S. Open at Cherry Hills in Denver in 1960. Joe never missed an 18-hole round of Arnie's at the Masters and was the leader of Arnie's Army. Joe had an azure blue Cadillac convertible, one of the last to roll off the line when Cadillac abandoned the convertible business. That became the defining symbol of our tailgate, and any fan of Arnie's was invited to be a part.

Marge Yuengling's husband's family owned the Yuengling Brewery in Pottsville, Pennsylvania. (It is the oldest brewery in the country.) She was a rabid Arnie fan and a loyal member of Arnie's gallery. Toward the end of Arnie's playing appearances at Augusta, both Marge and Colonel Joe needed to use motorized carts to attack Augusta National. Anyone who's been there knows that it is not a golf course for the faint of heart. But they persevered, and Arnie loved them for it. Marge is no longer with us, but her son Dick and his team of daughters have turned the brewery into something big-time. They too are Arnie fans.

Doc Murphey from Roanoke Rapids, North Carolina, quarterbacked the football team at Wake Forest when Arnie was there. In his coat, tie, and straw hat, he religiously followed Arnie every April in Augusta. And at the conclusion of a round, he pontificated at every tailgating event, telling shaggy-dog stories that rivaled those of any storyteller in length and hilarity. He was one of a kind.

Arnie at the Tailgate

Obviously, tailgating at the Masters was a big part of our trip to Augusta every year. 1989 was Arnie's 35th Masters, and I got a call from Dick Taylor, the editor of *Golf World*. Dick said that the sportswriters had gotten a silver plate to present to Arnie to commemorate the occasion. Dick asked me to call Arnie and invite him to our tailgate, where they would present their gift. As people passed our tailgate, they couldn't believe that Arnie was there in the midst of his Army. That was the best tailgate we ever had.

Here I am photographing this historic event. Pictured are Dick Taylor, Arnie, and Delvin Miller.

Some of the hard-core fans (from left): Kitty Morris, Pat Richter, Susie Meeks, and Pete Richter, along with Arnie, Winnie, and Carolyn.

Arnie's 60th Birthday

Arnie's 60th was celebrated in style in September 1989 at the Bay Hill Club. Attending were many dear friends, golfers, and celebrities, including Bryant Gumbel and Kathleen Sullivan of NBC *Today Show* fame. B.J. Thomas played golf with the group and thrilled everyone with his rendition of "Happy Birthday."

A month later at the Bay Hill Member-Guest, a follow-up birthday celebration was held close to Halloween, and guests were asked to come in costume. The King came dressed as B.J. Thomas; Dow and Linda Finsterwald were disguised as President Reagan and wife Nancy.

Arnie celebrating with NBC anchors Bryant Gumbel and Kathleen Sullivan, who both love golf.

B.J. Thomas (a.k.a. Arnie) and Ronald and Nancy Reagan (a.k.a. Dow and Linda Finsterwald).

Here's the golfing group on Arnie's birthday (left to right): Howdy, Russ Meyer, Kathleen, Arnie, Cliff Benson, B.J. Thomas, and Ken Bowman.

THE 1990s

THE KING phased down tournament competition and endured serious personal and family illnesses, including the loss of Winnie Palmer in 1999.

AND I, along with my family, socialized with the Palmers. We had dinner with Barbara and Jack Nicklaus and spent the day with Pres. George H.W. Bush at Caves Valley Golf Club. Our daughters got married. Tragedy struck when Winnie left us.

To the PGA Tour players, Arnie is the icing on the cake.

Peter Jacobson's Cake

During the 1991 Bay Hill Invitational, Arnie made the cut, and Peter Jacobson bought a cake to celebrate the occasion. During a rain delay on Saturday, he called Arnie's office and asked him to come down to the locker room. No press was allowed, just Doc Giffin and me—and I took all the photos. Arnie personally cut every player a piece of cake with tears in his eyes.

*** The Orlando Sentinel, Monday, March 18, 1991   C-7

Let him eat cake

Peter Jacobsen (right) ambushes Arnold Palmer with a surprise tribute from the players Sunday at Bay Hill. The presentation is made in the locker room during a rain delay at the Nestle Invitational. Jacobsen: 'The players have such respect and admiration for Arnold. We just wanted to show that.'

PHOTO/HOWDY GILES

The local Orlando Sentinel *reports the event, using my photograph.*

Here's the story in Peter Jacobson's own words:

When Arnold made the cut in his own event, the 1991 Bay Hill Classic, I felt it was only right that we all reward him for that accomplishment and thank him for a great week at the same time. So after play on Friday, I stopped by the local bakery and asked how quickly I could get a sheet cake that would serve about 75. I was told it would take three days. I also said I wanted to have the tournament logo and a personal message in icing on the cake. He said *that* would take a week. Then I told the baker I needed it the next day. He said "No chance, not possible." When I told him it was for Arnold Palmer, he didn't hesitate and said, "I'll see you at 8:00 AM tomorrow morning."

When I arrived at Bay Hill that next morning, I asked the locker room staff to put this good-sized sheet cake somewhere close but out of sight. I explained that I wanted to present it to Arnold at some point over the weekend when the time was right. But with players teeing off from 8:00 AM to 2:00 PM both days, I wasn't sure when that "right time" would be.

As luck would have it (or maybe it was divine intervention?) a huge thunderstorm rolled through the golf course, drenching it with rain. Luckily for me, we had a delay in that day's play, bringing everyone off the golf course and into the locker room together. What perfect timing! It gave me a great opportunity to present the cake to Arnold.

When I was sure all of the players were present, I called for everyone's attention, asked Arnold to come up, and I presented him the cake on behalf of all of the players. I thanked him for another fantastic opportunity to play at Bay Hill, for all of his hard work and commitment on our behalf, and I congratulated him on making the cut. But I also pointed out that because he owned the place and had been redesigning the course for years, he *should* make the cut since he knew every blade of grass and all the shortcuts!

Everyone cheered, came up, and thanked Arnold. I pulled out a knife and made Arnold take the first piece. He cut the rest of the cake, and we all devoured it.

The rain delay lasted about two hours, so we had the chance to hang out, eat some cake, dry off, and talk to Arnold. As a young player, one of the cherished times on Tour is when you can get five to 10 minutes to talk one-on-one with one of the game's legends, like Palmer, Nicklaus, Watson, Trevino, or Player. This was one of those times. Arnold sat in the locker room and held court, telling stories and recalling great moments in his career and in others', keeping all of us players spellbound. These times with someone like Arnold are rare, and I'm sure everyone who was in that locker room has never forgotten that time with Arnold, that rain delay, or that cake. I haven't.

Meeting a President

Arnie was a guest of President George Herbert Walker Bush in April 1992 for a round of golf at the prestigious Caves Valley Golf Club outside Baltimore. Arnie invited me along, and he knew I had arrived before he did when he saw the press and pros all wearing umbrella pins. (I always carried many to distribute.) I joined them in a private room where Arnie introduced me as his friend, dentist, and photographer. The president replied that I had been a topic of conversation at the previous night's dinner. How great is that? The president talking about Howdy Giles! I had lunch with them and walked the course with them in a foursome that included Griffin Bell, secretary of state, and Reg Murphey, past president of the USGA and a member of Cave's Valley. I took hundreds of photos that day.

President Bush sent along the following to accompany this book:

"We Bushes share the worldwide respect for Arnold Palmer the golfer, and we treasure our friendship with Arnold Palmer the man."

—FORMER PRESIDENT GEORGE H.W. BUSH

Arnie introducing Howdy.

The people in these photos need no identification.

The press was not allowed on the playing grounds for security reasons, but a Newsweek *photographer took this picture from afar to accompany this magazine article.*

PERISCOPE

Sorry, press corps, no more TV tee offs: Bush golfing last month

THE PRESIDENT

Can We Play Through?

White House physician Dr. Burton Lee may have prescribed more vacation time for George Bush to relieve presidential stress. But senior campaign strategists are discouraging Bush from manic rounds of his favorite elitist pastimes, golf and boating—particularly at his vacation home in Maine. As they did in '88, aides worry that photos of Bush in a golf cart or in his Cigarette speed boat reinforce the image of an aristocratic president out of touch with the common man. Yet Bush's men know better than to try to keep him off the links, so they will try to limit photos of him at play. When Bush and his houseguest, Arnold Palmer, recently helicoptered from Camp David for a round at the posh Caves Valley Golf Club northwest of Baltimore, the White House banned coverage of the president teeing off. Photos were allowed only at the end of the game. ∎

RELIGION

Falwell Woes

You remember Jerry Falwell, the once omnipresent televangelist. Although untouched by scandal himself, Falwell had to sell off his cable-TV network after the preacher-gate scandals of the late 1980s hurt business for all televangelists. Now Falwell's flagship creation, Liberty University in Lynchburg, Va., is in trouble. Falwell must settle creditor claims for $60 million lent to Liberty or close the doors on its 5,000 students. Still, the zealous preacher is confident he

CAMPAIGN '92

Half Bakered

George Bush's campaign chairman, Robert Mosbacher, apparently worried that the president's re-election effort is floundering, last week turned to Bush confidant and top political strategist Secretary of State James Baker. On Sunday, Mosbacher invited Baker to play a round of golf, administration sources say. After the outing, the sources say, a shaken Mosbacher told aides he intended to put in longer hours, seven days a week, to get the campaign on track. "Baker read him the riot act," says a top Bush aide. "He said the White House has failed to communicate the simplest idea, the simplest proposal." Mosbacher told NEWSWEEK the "two old friends" had talked, but he denied Baker was critical of the campaign "in any way."

'Shaken': Mosbacher, Baker

CONVENTIONAL WISDOM WATCH

Rich Ballplayers Edition

Remember all those multimillion-dollar contract signings during the off season? The CW, as jaundiced about sports as politics, looks at who's earning the bucks and who's not.

MEGASTARS

	Conventional Wisdom
Bobby Bonilla ⬇	Batting .153 at Shea, .234 overall, 2 HRs. You call these $29 million stats?
Ryne Sandberg ⬇	Traditional slow starter, but .261 and 4 HRs? Business as usual at Wrigley.
Frank Viola ↔	Life in Boston seems to agree with him, but beware second-half El Foldo.
Jack Morris ▲	The big-game pitcher the Jays have

WASHINGTON FAX

Power Play

The big winner—White House division—in President Bush's decision to attend the eco summit in Rio next month is domestic-poli czar **Clayton Yeutter**. H pushed hard for Bush go, ignoring "very emo tional assaults" from budget director **Richar Darman** and White House counsel **C. Boyd Gray**, White House sources say. Darman a Gray, the sources say, gued that the summit treaty would be very costly and would alien ate big business and key to Bush's re-electio With the help of top Sta Department officials, Yeutter negotiated co promise treaty langua that Bush accepted. D man denies that he an Yeutter disagreed.

POLITICS

An Upset in Alabama?

Until recently, Alabam Richard Shelby was co ing toward re-election. N first-term Democrat is w about a primary challen Chris McNair, a former s legislator and father of o the four girls killed in th Birmingham church bom One recent poll showed M ahead by 48 percent to 4 cent. McNair backers hop anger among women vot over Shelby's vote for Su Court Justice Clarence T as will help spark an ups Carol Braun's March wi Sen. Alan Dixon in the I primary.

Sudden challenge: McNai

Although no one is allowed to the back of the 12th hole during tournament play, during this practice round I was able to take this shot of Arnie from a bunker there.

Augusta 1992

The Saturday prior to the 1992 Masters, Arnie invited me to fly with him to Augusta to take some photos during a practice round. After we arrived, Arnie asked Mr. Jack Stephens, the new president of Augusta National, to join him for 18, but he was unable to do so and suggested I sub for him. Arnie gave me that don't-you-dare look, and I declined, but I did take more than 300 photos.

Arnie and me with Mr. Jack Stephens, who followed us from the 13th hole into the clubhouse during this practice round.

Arnie off the 1ˢᵗ tee at Cherry Hills in the 1993 Senior Open.

Back at Cherry Hills

This photo of Arnie hitting off the 1st tee during the Senior Open in 1993 at Cherry Hills Golf Course brings to mind Arnie's earlier bid in 1960 to win the U.S. Open at the same venue. At that time, Bob Drum was a famous syndicated sports columnist from Pittsburgh, Pennsylvania, who was a good friend of Arnie's and was working the 1960 event. Going into the final round, Drum made what was perhaps a mistake in telling Arnie he had no chance to win because he was seven shots off the lead when he teed off. That lit a fire in Arnie. He birdied the first hole and four of the first five holes, and Drum made his way into Arnie's gallery. The two remained friends, and this photo of the two of them was taken in Augusta at the Masters many years later.

Arnie and syndicated sports columnist Bob Drum, an old friend.

The Galas

Arnie has always believed in "giving back." He made Orlando, Florida's Arnold Palmer Hospital and the Winnie Palmer Hospital for Women and Children the beneficiaries of contributions from his Bay Hill Invitational.

Also, the Latrobe Hospital benefited from Golf Galas, which Arnie staged each year from 1993 to 1997, at which very well-known Tour players participated, along with CEOs of industry and golfing friends who wished to contribute to the very worthwhile cause. I was lucky enough to attend each of these galas and rub shoulders with and take photos of the cream of the crop of the golfing world.

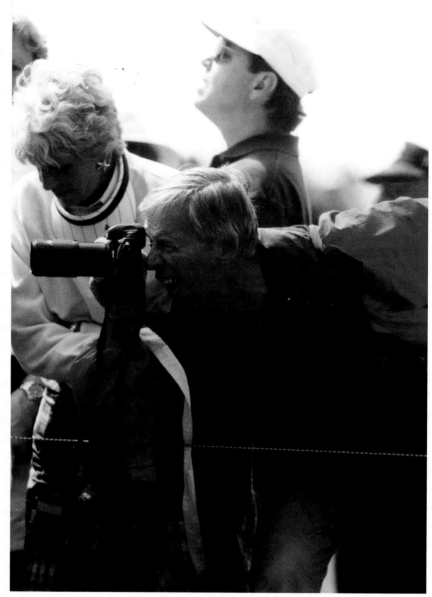

Guess who is taking photos at one of these galas?

When Arnold won his first Masters, I was a young caddy at a club in northwestern Pennsylvania. The notion that we would become friends decades later was as illusory as my becoming a scratch golfer. We first met long after all those Tour victories, but our friendship has given me the opportunity to learn, admire, and truly enjoy all those personal qualities that have made him so special. I don't think he'll mind that I make a few private moments public.

He addressed the Past Champions Dinner before the Bay Hill tournament several years ago. His message was simple and from the heart. He reminded the players that their profession revolved around a game that offered them an unbelievable lifestyle. He exhorted them to never forget that without sponsors, fans, and volunteers, they would just be playing a game.

A couple of years ago I watched Arnold hit a spectacular shot out of a water hazard. As he sat down in the cart, he actually answered the unspoken question I had written all over my face.

"It's only mud and water, and it will dry."

I couldn't resist asking why he didn't take an unplayable. It was a nice day, a casual round with friends. What was the point?

He smiled and observed, "I hit it, didn't I? Then it wasn't unplayable."

On a magnificent fall day a few years back, we stopped in the middle of the fairway, and Arnold directed me to look around and enjoy the beautiful scenery. As we gazed at the blue sky, a few clouds, and the multicolored landscape, he volunteered, "This is my office. Now you can understand why I like to go to work every day."

Of course, in his office, living room, or in a restaurant, Arnold is the same person. With corporate executives, political figures, the locker-room attendant, or the autograph-seeking fan, Arnold is the same person. You may think he is special—he doesn't. He is the son of Doris and Deacon. I am the son of Laura and Tom. We play golf, laugh at each other's jokes, pose for photos for Howdy Giles, talk politics, sports, business, have an occasional adult beverage, and enjoy the unique intersection of our lives and worlds. We are friends. It just doesn't get any better than that.

—TOM RIDGE

1993 Gala: (from left) Chi Chi Rodriguez, Dow Finsterwald, Arnie, and Curtis Strange.

At the 1994 Gala (left to right): Arnie, Jay Haas, Jack Nicklaus, Howdy, and Peter Jacobson.

Arnie with Jim and Sharon Rohr. Jim is CEO of Pittsburgh-based PNC Bank, a major sponsor of the Galas.

The 1995 Gala (left to right): Fuzzy Zoeller, Arnie, Lee Trevino, and Gary Player.

The 1996 Gala (left to right): Arnie, Greg Norman, Rocco Mediate, and Dave Marr.

The 1997 Gala (from left): Howdy, Tiger Woods, Cook Griffith, Arnie, Bill Joyner, Tom Lehman, Cliff Benson, and Davis Love III.

AT&T Pro-Am

My photo of Arnie and astronaut Alan Shepard at the AT&T Pro-Am. In return, Shepard sent me the photo of him hitting a golf ball on the moon. Cool!

To HOWDY GILES —
It's all a big sand (lunar dust) trap!
Alan Shepard   2/6/71

"Howdy and Arnold's relationship strikes me as being really unique in sports and says something great about both men. Without question, for just about every reason I can think of, Arnold Palmer is golf's greatest ambassador, not to mention the game's most appealing figure. He's also one of the most gracious and classiest guys you'll ever meet–a quality he extends to everyone. Arnold is so authentic. And that's the key to his vast popularity around the world. I think modern athletes in every game could learn a world of things from just watching him operate. His relationship with Howdy speaks volumes about the respect Arnold has for his fans and the game. It evolved from honest admiration into a deep friendship, the kind of wonderful thing we could all imagine happening with Arnold Palmer."

—JIM NANTZ

Huey Lewis and Jim Nantz (CBS Sports) at the 1996 AT&T Pro-Am: two guys who really, really love golf.

Arnie spoke to the assembled group with fond memories of his years in Augusta filling his mind. It was an emotional occasion.

ARNOLD PALMER

Arnold Palmer Day, April 4, 1995, at Augusta

Jack Stephens, the president of Augusta National, presided over the presentation of a plaque honoring Arnie on the occasion proclaimed Arnold Palmer Day, April 4, 1995, at Augusta National.

Arnie, Winnie, and Jack Stephens.

The 1996 Masters

Arnie played a practice round with Tiger Woods and Jack Nicklaus at the 1996 Masters. To get near enough to get photos of the group, I had to position myself three holes ahead of them.

A dynamic golfing trio tees it up together during a practice round at the '96 Masters.

Sarah Strange looks on as Arnie signs autographs. Her sons caddied the
Par-3 tournament for their father Curtis and Tom Kite.

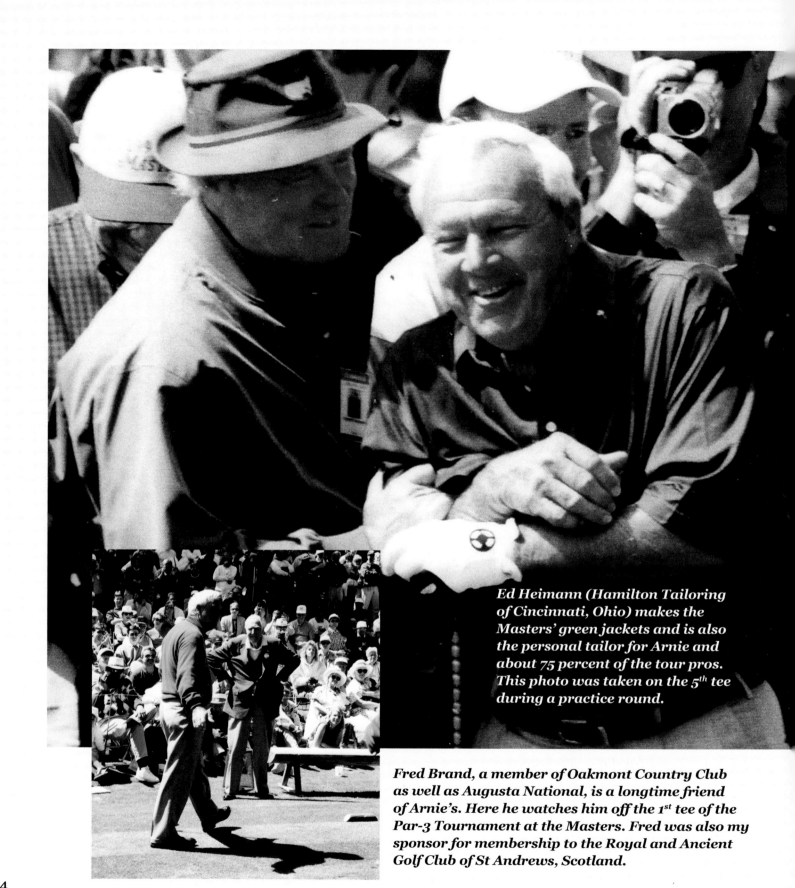

Ed Heimann (Hamilton Tailoring of Cincinnati, Ohio) makes the Masters' green jackets and is also the personal tailor for Arnie and about 75 percent of the tour pros. This photo was taken on the 5th tee during a practice round.

Fred Brand, a member of Oakmont Country Club as well as Augusta National, is a longtime friend of Arnie's. Here he watches him off the 1st tee of the Par-3 Tournament at the Masters. Fred was also my sponsor for membership to the Royal and Ancient Golf Club of St Andrews, Scotland.

2004 and 2006 Masters Winner

Phil Mickelson

In 1991 Phil Mickelson had written Arnold Palmer a letter to see if he could play a practice round with Arnie, and he agreed. I flew to the Masters with Arnie and took many photos of both men playing that round of golf. While I was at the Walker Cup later that year, I gave copies of those photos to Phil, which he enjoyed very much, and he asked me for my business card. Three weeks later, I got a handwritten note from the then-19-year-old thanking me for my photographs.

Arnie and Phil Mickelson.

Dinner at 8:00 PM for our group of six (Carolyn was the photographer for this one).

June 1996 Senior PGA Tour Tournament, Chester Valley Country Club

For a number of years, my daughter Julie worked for Mary Ann Saleski in the Philadelphia area, staging golf events. In June 1996 they were in charge of a Senior PGA Tour event at the Chester Valley Country Club in Malvern, Pennsylvania. While there, Carolyn and I were invited to join Arnie and Winnie and Jack and Barbara Nicklaus for a dinner for six. It was an unforgettable evening—and of course I had my camera in tow.

The event moved to the Hartefeld Country Club outside Wilmington, Delaware, where Davis Sezna was the owner.

Davis, my good friend who always keeps us laughing, had this to say: "Howdy has always provided me with great comedic material, but where would we be without Howdy's heart and timely photographs of Arnold's world...even though using Arnold's dental X-rays as a Christmas card was a bit over the top."

Dick Vermeil, former head coach of the Philadelphia Eagles, is a golf fan and had a chance to see Arnie during the tournament.

Arnie, Davis Sezna, and Jack Nicklaus.

Arnie took this photo of me, John Bannon, and Steve Myers during a golf round at Latrobe after we flew in with his birthday cake.

Arnie, John, and I admire the wooden statue of Arnie's father "Deke" carved from an old wooden tree trunk on the Latrobe course.

A Coconut Cake, "Leaving on a Jet Plane"

Winnie called me in September 1996 to ask a favor of me. (I loved it when she did.) Arnie's birthday was coming, and she wanted to treat him to his favorite coconut cake from Bookbinders in Philadelphia, but they were unable to send it. Did I have any ideas? Did I! A friend of mine named John Bannon desperately wanted to play golf with Arnie, and a friend of John's named Steve Myers had a jet. The idea was for them to fly to Wilmington to pick up me and the cake and then fly on to Latrobe for a round of golf. Aboard the plane I said to Steve, "You're not going to believe how much the cake cost." And he gave me a look back and replied, "And you are not going to believe what it cost me to fly to Delaware to pick up you and this cake!" Laughs all around!

Arnie with quarterback Bernie Kosar and "Da Coach," Mike Ditka.

Arnold the Sports Fan

Arnie is not only into golf, but he likes all sports. Here he is with some famous sporting figures.

Greg Maddux and John Smoltz, both Atlanta Braves pitchers playing in the Bay Hill Shootout.

Arnie and Howdy with three-time National League MVP Mike Schmidt, Philadelphia Phillies third baseman.

Arnie welcomes Peyton Manning to his tournament.

Hall of Fame first baseman Stan Musial and Arnie during play at the Isleworth Country Club Pro-Am in Windemere, Florida.

Tiger teeing off on 18.

Arnie and Tiger (with Howdy) Take to the Bay Hill Fairway

On the Saturday before Tiger was to play his first Masters as a pro, I was scheduled to play with Arnie in the Shootout at Bay Hill. I asked who our partner would be, and Arnie replied, "Tiger Woods." Tiger wanted to pick Arnie's brain as to how to function with the gallery and autographs and so on. Tiger was in training for Augusta. The day before, at his home course Isleworth, near Bay Hill, he had shot 59 playing with Mark O'Meara.

I stopped by my condo to tell Carolyn of my good fortune, and she told me not to be obnoxious with my camera. For five holes I kept it under wraps. I started thinking, *This is pretty dumb. How many people get to play golf in a group with Arnie and Tiger?* So I began to click away, and no one seemed bothered.

The three of us on the 16th tee.

Spider and Arnie

Spider Miller had won the USGA Mid-Amateur in 1996, which meant he would be playing at the Masters in '97. In February he called and asked how he might contact Arnie to ask it they could play a practice round together in Augusta. I suggested he write to Arnie, saying he had spoken to me. Spider is a friend of Fuzzy Zoeller, and at the Bay Hill Tournament in March, Fuzzy and I asked Arnie who he was playing with at the practice round in Augusta. Arnie replied, "Howdy's friend, Spider Miller." It worked! Arnie and Spider are now very good friends.

"How do you describe a man who is your hero, best friend, life counselor, flying mentor, and golfing buddy? I suppose the best way to summarize my feelings for Arnie is to relate my observation that all people have when they see him, whether in a tournament gallery, a restaurant, an airport, or business meeting. The experience and effect is always the same, *a big smile.*"
—SPIDER MILLER

Spider Miller, Arnie, and Howdy.

(Second from right) Spider Miller ('96 USGA Mid-Am champ) playing a practice round in Augusta with three golfing greats, Jack, Fuzzy, and Arnie.

Arnie Becomes a Shutterbug

A Nikon moment.

The teeth look good, but I don't know about the swing!

Check out this lens!

John Clouse, who has provided me with the latest Nikon cameras for years, and Arnie.

Arnie's 70th Birthday

To celebrate Arnie's 70th birthday in September 1999, Winnie orchestrated a three-day event at Latrobe Country Club. Friends flew in from all over, and there was much golf and many tributes in Arnie's honor. Tom Ridge, the governor of Pennsylvania at the time (and since secretary of Homeland Security for the Bush White House following 9/11) spoke at a moving ceremony at which the Latrobe Airport was rededicated as the Arnold Palmer Airport. Mark McCormack and Alistair Johnson made a presentation from IMG. Arnie's brother Jerry and sisters Lois Jean and Sandy were there, as were daughters Peg and Amy and their husbands and seven of their children.

The night's event was held in the totally reconstructed barn on the premises of Latrobe, and what a monument it is to what Winnie thinks a restoration should be. (The famous artist David Armstrong was commissioned to do the signature portrait of the renovated structure.) Winnie had not been well, and this was her last public appearance. But the memories of her last big party will forever live in the hearts of those who were there.

Arnie and his special friends at his party (left to right): John Harris, Russ Meyer, Dave Roderick, Arnie, Dick Ferris, Howard Fox, Tom O'Brian, and Tom Ridge.

More friends (left to right): Pat Richter, Howard Fox, Becky Fischer, Dave Roderick, Yvonne Fox, Tom Ridge, Arnie, Carolyn, Pete Richter, and me.

Arnie celebrates with sisters Lois Jean and Sandy and brother Jerry.

Arnie with daughter Amy's children (left to right): Sam, Emily, Annie, and Katie.

Mark McCormack was truly the pioneer of the sports marketing industry. Early on, he envisioned the charismatic Arnold Palmer with lucrative endorsement contracts. Their partnership, sealed on a handshake, was a win-win situation for them both. Today, every athlete who signs a multimillion-dollar endorsement contract owes a debt of gratitude to Arnie and Mark.

Mark McCormack with Arnie as he's about to cut the cake at his 70th birthday party.

Early on, Arnie was Mark's sole client. But when Mark's International Management Group grew to epic size, Alistair Johnson, a Glasgow native with an accounting background, was brought on board in the '70s to personally oversee Arnie's businesses. Arnie's empire continued to grow under Alistair's expert guidance.

Alistair Johnson presents Arnie with a commemorative book given by IMG.

Arnie's Friends and Business Associates

Alistair Johnson, Arnie, and Barry Hyde, formerly a marketing executive with MasterCard (and lead sponsor of the Arnold Palmer Invitational). Barry now works in a similar position with the USGA.

Another one of Arnie's advisors, Charlie Meachem says this about his good friend Arnie:

"Shortly after I retired as commissioner of the LPGA at the end of 1995, Arnie asked me to become one of his personal business advisors. I have acted in that capacity ever since. Although I have very much enjoyed my work with Arnie, by far the most rewarding part of the experience is the deep personal friendship that has grown between us. As this picture shows, that friendship and warmth includes our wives as well."

Marilyn Meachem, Arnie, Kit, and Charlie.

Arnie has many friends and business associates, but there are two that deserve special mention: Russ Meyer and Dick Ferris.

Next to golf, Arnie greatest love is flying. Russ Meyer helped him purchase his first plane. A very fine attorney, he left law to head an aviation company. He was so successful that by 1975 he was chairman and CEO of Cessna Aviation. The Citation jet became a major company, and Arnie has owned six of them to date. Russ and his wife Helen have traveled extensively with the Palmers and were invited to be their guests every year in Augusta. Arnie could probably write a book on experiences he and Russ have shared.

Arnie and Russ in front of N1AP.

Arnie and I first met in the summer of 1961 in Cleveland. He had recently earned his pilot's license, and one of my initial assignments as a young attorney was to negotiate the purchase of his first aircraft. We discovered during this process that we shared a passion for both golf and aviation, among other common interests, and our close friendship now spans almost 50 years.

Our adventures during those years included a record-setting transatlantic flight in the Citation X from Latrobe to St. Andrews. Arnie is an exceptionally skilled aviator with more than 17,000 flight hours. He is very much at home in the left seat of the Citation X. If he hadn't been such a great golfer, he would likely have pursued a career in aviation.

Spending the week in Augusta with Arnie and Winnie during practically every Masters remains among our warmest memories. And playing as his partner in the AT&T was an unbelievable treat.

—RUSS MEYER

Dick Ferris is an entrepreneur extraordinaire, but he is also a rabid competitor on the golf course, something Arnie appreciates, as they are often playing partners at Bay Hill. (Dick and his wife Kelsey have a winter home in the area.) Dick is the former chairman of United Airlines and was a major force in having the Hertz Corporation as the major sponsor of Arnie's Bay Hill tournament for many years. Dick also heads the policy board for the PGA Tour. Talking about his friend Arnie, Dick said, "Friend, teacher, and business partner, through thick and thin, Arnold defines the meaning of friendship."

Arnie and Dick Ferris waiting their turn.

Arnie's friend John Harris from
Charlotte, North Carolina, brought Arnie
to Charlotte, where they have many
business interests together.

Arnie's stockbroker, Dick Connolly, pictured
here with Tom Ridge and Howdy. Maybe it was
Yellow Shirt Day!

Joe Gibbs and Arnie.

"Arnold and I met in 1990 at Shoal Creek as
a result of Winnie and Arnold staying in my
guesthouse during the PGA Championship. We
became friends and later business partners as
cofounders of the Golf Channel. I became very
enamored with Arnold Palmer "the man," not
"the icon." The way Arnold treats people and
conducts his life is a guiding light to me and so
many other people the world over. Being his
friend for so many years has led to experiences
with him and golf that I will treasure for the rest
of my life. Winnie Palmer once said to me that
Arnold was just a very nice man—and I agree
completely."

— JOE GIBBS

Hollis Cavner runs many golf tournaments, and Arnie has been very loyal, trying to compete in as many as possible. When asked about Arnie, Hollis said, "Having a pal like Arnie is truly the greatest honor I could ever hope for. I have never understood why he took a liking to me and has helped me so much in my career and starting my business and with great advice when I need it. To me, he is not the King because he won 62 events on Tour."

Arnie and Hollis Cavner.

The King is still smiling after 18 holes of the Seminole Pro-Member, but not nearly as much as playing partners Tim Neher, Seth Waugh, and PGA Tour Player Brad Faxon." —SETH WAUGH

"The first time I met Arnold was in 1984 at the Players Championship at TPC Sawgrass, and we were paired together on Sunday with Peter Jacobsen early in the day. I was nervous and excited and couldn't wait to play with him. On that crowded 1st hole, Arnie outdrove both of us and kind of let us have it! He told me on the 2nd hole that he was probably going to quit playing competitively that year…and that was 28 years ago. He also told me to make eye contact with people and they won't forget you. Nobody was ever better at that than him. I cannot imagine the game of golf without Arnold Palmer." —BRAD FAXON

(Left to right) Tim Neher, Arnie, Seth Waugh, and Brad Faxon.

Doc Giffin.

Arnie and Cori Britt.

Doc Giffin is Arnie's longtime personal assistant, and one could not find a more loyal friend and employee. Everything that goes to Arnold Palmer goes through Doc.

More recently, Cori Britt has been handling much of Arnie's work in Florida and many times is the handsome caddy who has been with Arnie at golf tournaments. Arnie's secretary Gina Barrone has been with him for years in Latrobe, and Janet Hulcher keeps his affairs straight in Florida.

Gina Barrone in Latrobe.

Janet Hulcher in Orlando.

When in Palm Springs, where Arnie also has a home, he is seen with various members of the "Rat Pack." Ernie Dunleavy lives in Bermuda Dunes, Palm Springs, and was the former Chairman of the Bob Hope Desert Classic for more than 30 years. David Chapman was the developer-owner of the Tradition Golf Club in Palm Springs. Arnie loves the desert, and David convinced Arnie that this was the ideal spot to open the Arnold Palmer Restaurant featuring Palmer (Luna) wines and Arnie's all-time favorite entries, such as meat loaf and macaroni and cheese. During high season, reservations need to be made months in advance.

The late Ed Seay was executive vice president of the Palmer Course Design Company from 1979 until 2008. Ed and Arnie traveled all over the world designing and visiting golf courses. Ed probably spent nearly as much time on the N1AP as Arnie did.

The Rat Pack: Arnie, Ed Seay, Ernie Dunleavy, and David Chapman.

Arnie and David Chapman at the Arnold Palmer Restaurant.

Arnie and Ed Seay enjoying a good story.

THE 2000s

THE KING was recognized as the game's elder statesman as honors such as the Presidential Medal of Freedom in 2004 came one after another.

AND I attended my last consecutive Masters in 2004; it was Arnie's 50th. (We both returned again in 2009.) Our friends, my daughters and their husbands, and now our grandchildren, enjoy being with Arnie.

Arnie designed a nine-hole golf course in Augusta, Georgia, for use in the First Tee Program. Here, he cuts the ribbon for the official course opening.

Arnie Giving Back

Arnie is very active in the USGA's First Tee Program, which encourages less-privileged youngsters to try their hands at golf.

Arnie at the 2000 Senior Tournament at Jasna Polana speaking to the First Tee Program participants.

Arnie and Joe Louis Barrow, son of the late, great boxer, who attended this special event.

(Left to right) Buzz Taylor, Arnie, and Jim Hand.

Golf is and always has been a major part of Arnie's life. Through golf he has met and become friends with many others for whom golf is also a major focus. Arnie and President Ford in 1974 started the USGA Amateur Program to encourage golfers everywhere to join the group and support their cause. Buzz Taylor and Jim Hand, both former presidents of the USGA, are special friends of Arnie's. Through the USGA, Arnie has made many other friends as well, including John Staver. John is a wizard on the rules of golf and was instrumental in designing the *Decisions on the Rules of Golf* to be made smaller so that the rules officials would be able to carry the book during competitions. John is a member of many famous golf clubs as well, including Pine Valley, Merion, Seminole, and the Royal and Ancient Golf Club of St. Andrews, Scotland, to name a few. John has worked many major USGA events over the years.

Arnie and Tom Meeks.

Tom Meeks, the former head of rules and competition for the USGA, was front and center at Arnie's final U.S. Open at Oakmont in 1994. Tom was also in charge of the scorers' tent in Augusta for Arnie's final Masters in 2004.

Tom & Laurel Loss with Arnie.

Dr. Tom Loss and wife Laurel are also close friends of Arnie's through the USGA. Tom is a member of the USGA Mid-Am Committee. Also a top rules official for the organization, Tom has worked many U.S. Opens, Senior Opens and U.S. Amateurs. Tom is also involved with helping CBS with the rules on TV.

Arnie with Carolyn and Bob Hooper.

Another special friendship Arnie has cultivated along the way is with Dr. Bob and Carolyn Hooper. Bob has been a member of the Mid-Am Committee of the USGA since it started in 1982. Bob has worked every Mid-Am tournament—and many U.S. Opens, Senior Opens, and United States Amateurs. His wife, Carolyn, is a member of the Ladies Committee of the USGA. Carolyn has also worked many major events for the USGA, not only in the United States but also abroad. Bob is the head of the rules committee for the Palmer Cup that will be played at Cherry Hills in Denver in 2009, home of Arnie's lone U.S. Open title.

Sam gets a grip.

Sam takes a stance.

Arnie and His Grandchildren

The apple never falls far from the tree.

Arnie has been blessed with seven delightful grandchildren and is now even celebrating being a great-grandfather. His daughter Amy, her husband Roy, and their four children have always lived close to Bay Hill, which gave Arnie a chance to watch his grandson Sam grow up with golf. The photos here show Sam receiving instructions in the basics of the grip and stance. He was a medalist in the USGA Junior Amateur and played in the U.S. Amateur. He has also played with Arnie in the Father-Son tournament. He is a member of the Clemson University golf team and has won the Bay Hill Club Championship.

Arnie and Sam toasting their success in a tournament round.

Arnie with six of his grandchildren: (left to right) Emily, Annie, Sam, Katie, Will, and Anna.

Arnie with his great-grandchildren, Charlotte and Sam.

Here's my favorite photo of Arnie and Winnie. It was used for the cover of a magazine.

The Arnold Palmer Invitational

The Arnold Palmer Invitational, previously known as the Bay Hill Invitational, has been the highlight of our winter season for many years. Here are some of the memories.

Ben Crenshaw, former winner of the Bay Hill Invitational, shares his thoughts on Arnie:

I first watched Arnold Palmer at Oak Hills Country Club in San Antonio when I was 10 years old. It was the first professional tournament I had ever attended. If I remember correctly, Arnie was in the midst of winning three Texas Opens in a row, and boy, did he have that place spellbound, including my brother, my father, and me.

As my playing progressed, I got to play a nine-hole exhibition with Arnie in Wichita Falls, Texas, at our Texas-Oklahoma Junior Tournament. I will always remember his gentlemanly manners, his warm smile, and his genuine concern for our golf games. I feel so fortunate to have witnessed his exploits on the golf course, which are legendary. But the fact remains that whatever professional golfers today possess, they owe this wonderful man all the gratitude in the world.

I am really proud to know Arnold Palmer. He has always stood for the right things in golf.

Ben Crenshaw playing at Bay Hill.

Ben Crenshaw and Arnie admire Dow Finsterwald's drive at the Bay Hill Invitational.

Tom Ridge, hockey great Bobby Orr, Arnie, Walt Macnee, President of International Markets, MasterCard Worldwide.

Michael Jordan, Tom Ridge, and Howdy.

Yogi Berra and Arnie.

My most vivid memory of Arnold Palmer is from July 1995, although it's not the universal image that most people would recall from that historic summer. Arnold that year played in his final British Open, fittingly at St Andrews, the place where he'd reinvigorated the great championship 35 years earlier. As the world's most popular golfer in 1960, he came to the British Open at a time when many American golfers wouldn't…finished second to Kel Nagle…and then went on to win the next two Claret Jugs.

What most people likely remember from the summer of 1995 is Arnold, standing on the Swilican Bridge, wistfully waving good-bye (why do I think Howdy probably snapped a few frames of this tableau?). It's one of the more memorable images from his long and distinguished golfing life.

The image I remember most of Arnold from that summer, though, is one you won't find in any book or collection. It was a private and insignificant moment but one that spoke volumes to me about who the man is and what he represents.

The week after the Open, the *Senior* British Open was being played at Royal Port Rush in Northern Ireland. "The troubles," as they were euphemistically known, had vanquished significant championships from this golf-rich land for more than four decades, but now, with much fanfare, they had returned.

Port Rush is a brutish and rolling links, almost universally revered, but with its unassuming one-story clubhouse, it has the unpretentious feel of a "muni." When I got to the course on Tuesday, I pulled into the parking lot, and the first thing I saw was an image that I can still recall today as if it's right before my eyes.

There was Arnold Palmer, a man who counted kings and presidents as friends—a man who'd made millions and flew his own jet—sitting in the open trunk of his car, putting on his shoes…just like the rest of us do. I'm sure he didn't think anyone was watching. Why would anyone care?

It's often said that Arnold is a man of the people, and having spent a good deal of time around him over the last 20 years, I know that's not only true but is also a genuine and sincere part of his being. Thousands of words have been written expressing the sentiment. Every time I read them, my mind flashes back to that parking lot in Northern Ireland, and I understand that a picture truly is worth a thousand words, maybe more.

—JIMMY ROBERTS

Arnie and Chris McWilton, President, U.S. Markets, MasterCard Worldwide.

Arnie and Scott Wellington, current chairman of the Invitational.

Two longtime *huge* Arnie fans, Little Rock, Arkansas, natives, and close business associates/partners, John Reap, president of Town North Bank in Dallas and Bill Mathis, executive vice-president of MasterCard Worldwide at the Past Champions' Dinner.

(Left to right) John Reap, Arnie, and Bill Mathis.

Friends from Bay Hill

Dow and Linda Finsterwald have been at Bay Hill almost as long as Arnie.

"It was in the spring of 1948 that I first met Arnold Palmer. My introduction was a college golf match in which he played the front side in 29 strokes. For 60-plus years I have competed both against him and with him as a partner. I can't remember him ever being short or curt with anyone. Not that I am not a good person, but I do feel I am a better one because of having observed how he deals with people and in various situations. Arnold has the uncanny way of doing the right thing, not necessarily because it might result in some personal gain but simply because *it's the right thing to do.*"

—DOW FINSTERWALD

Look who's on the cover of SI!

Kit and Arnie with Linda and Dow Finsterwald.

Arnie practicing for his piano-playing debut.

Arnie, Kit, and Dick and Sharon Simmons.

Arnie's final performance.

Dick Simmons and his wife Sharon invited Arnie, Kit, Carolyn, and me to their beautiful home on the 18th green of Bay Hill to celebrate Dick's 70th birthday. Before dinner, Dick, who is an accomplished singer/musician, literally gleamed as he showed us his new toy—a player piano. This piece of musical equipment intrigued Arnie to no end. He loved playing it and commented to Kit that he planned to buy one, which he did. At the Bay Hill Invitational Pro-Am dinner, Arnie had his piano rolled into the club and placed at such an angle that no one knew that it was a player piano. Arnie was announced as the evening's entertainment, and he stunned people with his musical rendition. After a fashion, the guests realized they'd been had. But for Arnie, his toy was the hit of the night!

In the immediate vicinity of the Bay Hill Club there are seven condominium buildings that since the '70s and '80s have been home, especially in winter months, to Arnie, Winnie, Kit, and many of their longtime friends.

Howard and Yvonne Fox have been friends, coming to this area for 40-plus years. Howard, the former president of the Minnesota Twins, held spring training in the area for years. Yvonne is the Pearl Mesta of the group, hostessing parties where Arnie holds court among his friends.

Arnie, Kit, Yvonne and Howard Fox, and Howdy.

Dave Roderick is the former chairman and CEO of U.S. Steel in Pittsburgh, Arnie's old stomping ground. They are longtime friends. Dave and Becky Fischer live next door to Arnie in the summer in Latrobe and reside in the same condominium building in the winter. Dave was also instrumental in raising funds for a Latrobe memorial to Winnie following her death in 1999.

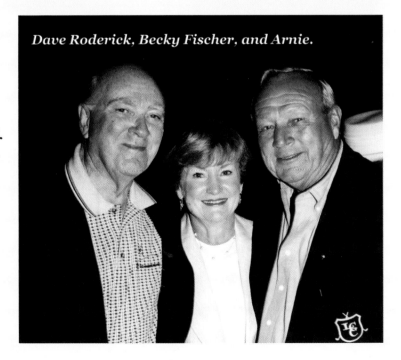

Dave Roderick, Becky Fischer, and Arnie.

Mary and Frank Gregor with Arnie.

Mary Gregor (with her late radiologist husband, Frank) is one of the few remaining original owners in the Bay Hill condos. She is an avid golfer, as are her children, who have now created a whole new generation of Arnie fans.

Pete and Pat Richter with Kit and Arnie.

Peter and Pat Richter are longtime friends of ours from dental school who took us on that fateful trip to Atlantic City in 1965, where I took the photo that essentially launched this book. We introduced the Richters to the Palmers, and all else is history—a history that includes following Arnie for four rounds in 100 or so Masters, U.S. Opens, PGA Championships, and other tournaments, as well as the purchase of a Bay Hill condo.

My sister Judy and her husband Dick were regular visitors to Bay Hill.

Bay Hill Shootout

The Bay Hill Shootout is quite famous. Members sign up to play daily and are paired with other club members as well as touring pros who may be members or guests of the club. Arnie is an avid member of the Shootout gang.

"It's all about the game, and the game at Arnie's Bay Hill Shootout is the best. Great golf course, competitive golf, and good friends—what more could you want?"

—BRUCE WALTERS

Arnie and Shootout partners Bruce Walters and Dick Ferris chew the fat while waiting to hit the next shot.

A good day for Arnie but not so for Bruce and Dick, as they open up their wallets.

Ron Jackson is the CEO of Meadowbrook Golf, which owns, manages, and maintains golf courses around the country. He and his wife Sylvia are members at Bay Hill, and Ron is a regular in the daily Shootout gang that routinely plays with Arnie.

"Arnold Palmer, a very special person with a very special passion, a passion for people. In travels all over the world and seeing world leaders in action, there is nobody that embodies the charm, the sincere interest in people like Arnold; it oozes out of him every minute of the day. The most fun, interesting people to be around in this world are people with a passion. My time with Arnold on the golf course has been special but no more special than the time off the course. There's only one King. He's motivated me in golf to keep playing, (Ron shoot your age) and in life that the shortest distance between two people is a smile. Arnold truly embodies a phrase I believe in: intelligent people know everything; powerful people know everybody! Arnold is truly powerful, he's special, and I am very proud of being Arnold's friend."

—RON JACKSON

Ron Jackson and Arnie.

Arnie, Eddie Merrins, and Bill Madonna.

"Arnie could hardly be Arnie without the engaging smile provided by Howdy Giles. It is a treat to know both gentlemen."

— EDDIE MERRINS

My Famous Photos

Every so often I go through my candid Arnie photos and send the best to Doc Giffin, Arnie's administrative assistant in the Latrobe office, to use in whatever way he sees fit. One such photo took on a life of its own, and it's one of my favorites. Arnie used it often when fans requested signed photos. Johnston & Murphy shoe company featured it in one of their ads. It was also pictured on the long boxes in which Arnold Palmer golf clubs were packaged and shipped. I was very flattered when LeRoy Neiman used it as a basis for a very well-known signed portrait that features Latrobe Country Club as a backdrop.

THE photo.

My personal favorite work of art, by LeRoy Neiman.

Rob Gillette, an executive with Marriott, designed and had painted a bottle of wine celebrating Arnie's 45th Masters participation and presented it to him in Augusta. It was another use of "the photo."

The close-up gives you a better look at the Arnold Palmer AriZona Tea can.

Rob Gillette, Arnie, and Howdy.

The Arnold Palmer AriZona Iced Tea can.

Arnie, Howdy, and Mark McCormack having a taste.

Happy 65th Birthday, Howdy

Over the years I have been lucky enough to attend birthday parties for Arnie on his 50th, 60th, and 70th. My 65th was a big one, and I wanted Arnie to be there. I asked David Chapman, owner of the Arnold Palmer restaurant in Palm Springs, to organize a party for me there. The evening is one I'll never forget.

Arnie and Kit arrive for my 65th birthday bash.

As the "honoree" I was not allowed to photograph anything. Subbing for me was my friend Joe Patterson of Los Angeles, who produced a beautiful scrapbook for me.

Of course, we wanted to use only Arnold Palmer wines at the event.

Howdy, Arnie, and Joe Patterson.

There were many Howdy and Arnie stories told at the party, and my friend Chip Eggers entertained the group with a howling comedy routine.

(Left to right) Chip Eggers, Arnie, Chip's son Riley, and Howdy.

Me, Carolyn, Arnie, and Kit at my 66th birthday.

Arnie, Kit, Carolyn, and me at my 67th birthday.

Wake Forest and the Masters

Arnie played college golf at Wake Forest University, and the university has always tugged at his heartstrings. Every year at the Masters in Augusta, Arnie cohosted a party with the administrators and alumni of the school. All players at the Masters who attended Wake were honored guests. Dr. Tom Hearn, the president of Wake Forest for many years, has hosted the party along with Arnie since the mid-'70s. Cliff Benson, a member of the Board of Trustees of Wake Forest, became a good friend of Arnie's over the years. Cliff played in the Wake Forest Pro-Ams for years and also attended many of Arnie's Latrobe Hospital Galas.

Arnie with Jesse Haddock, former Wake Forest golf coach.

Arnie with many past members of the Wake Forest golf team.

Cliff Benson with Arnie and me.

Arnie and Dick Tiddy, a golf teammate at Wake and longtime pro at Bay Hill.

Arnie at a Wake Forest commencement with president Tom Hearn.

Howdy, Kit, Arnie, and Rob Gillette.

In 2004 in order to commemorate Arnie's 50th Masters, there was a special ceremony at the Wake Forest party to honor Arnie. Rob Gillette presented Arnie with a hand-painted 50-pound magnum of wine.

At the same party, Julius Corpening and Jay Johnson (both Wake Forest alumni), presented Arnie with a painting by Doug London.

Jay Johnson and Julius Corpening unveiling the painting while the artist, Doug London, looks on.

This Masters was very special to me because it was Arnie's 50th.

Frank Chirkinian, CBS producer of the Masters, stops Arnie for a parking-lot chat.

The flowers are in bloom as Arnie walks to the 6th green.

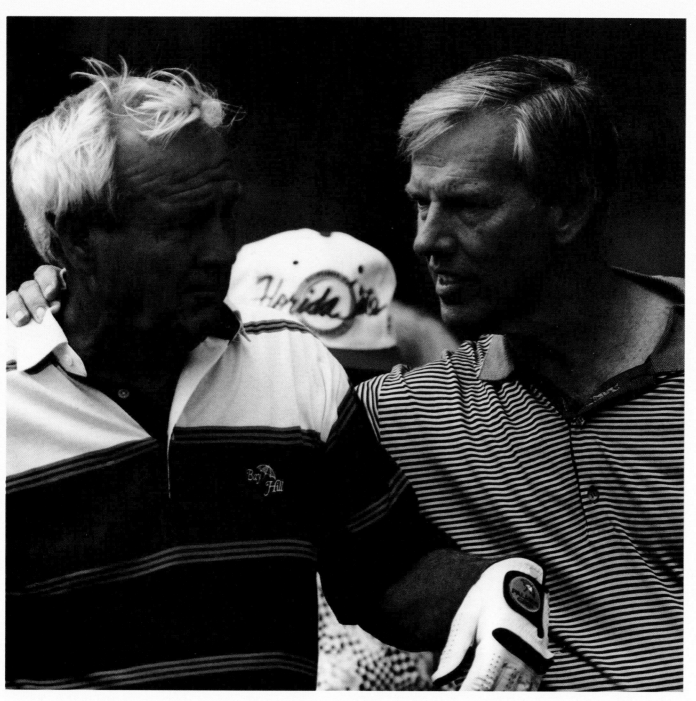

The King and I.

As always, the Army is still in force, even after 50 years.

As you see, this journey has enriched our lives immeasurably. I leave this book to our children, grandchildren, and the millions of Arnold Palmer fans around the world as a reminder that the King of golf will be with us forever.

Robin, David, and Giles Elliott.

Julie, Matthew, Cameron, Luke, and Lindsay Kelly.